THE

DARK

BETWEEN

STARS

Also by Atticus and available from Headline:

Love Her Wild

THE

DARK

BETWEEN

STARS

ATTICUS

poems

Headline

First published in Great Britain in 2018
by HEADLINE PUBLISHING GROUP

1

Photographs by Bryan Adam Castillo Photography, Poppet Penn, or released
under Creative Commons Zero license.

Interior design by Amy Trombat

Cataloguing in Publication Data is available from the British Library

Hardback ISBN 978 1 4722 5935 6

Printed and bound in Portugal by Printer Portuguesa

Headline's policy is to use papers that are natural, renewable and recyclable
products and made from wood grown in well-managed forests and other
controlled sources. The logging and manufacturing processes are expected
to conform to the environmental regulations of the country of origin.

HEADLINE PUBLISHING GROUP
An Hachette UK Company
Carmelite House
50 Victoria Embankment
London
EC4Y 0DZ

www.headline.co.uk
www.hachette.co.uk

For my mother,
for hiding poetry
where I'd find it.

'I loved you, so I drew these tides of men into my hands and wrote my will across the sky in stars . . .'

—T. E. Lawrence, *Seven Pillars of Wisdom*

THE

DARK

BETWEEN

STARS

STARS

For my part I know nothing with any certainty,
but the sight of the stars makes me dream.

—VINCENT VAN GOGH

He laughed,
my darling
you will never be unloved by me
you are too well tangled in my soul.

I don't know the truth of you
she whispered
but I have that feeling in my stomach
you get before your whole life changes.

Our love happened to us all at once
we had no time to think
we were caught up in the adventure of it
and hadn't a moment to spare.

The first time
I walked in Paris
there was a great remembering
of a thousand different dreams.

I woke before her
and she slept on as the sun rose
spilling light across our bed
she was an angel in my sheets
the girl I would draw
if given a thousand years
and only a promise
she might one day come to life.

THE

PRETTIEST

EYES

SPARKLE

FROM THE

INSIDE

OUT.

She was an endless source of
beautiful ideas and epiphanies
I wanted to live forever
in the quiet inspiration
of her existence.

In the mornings
she taught me French
and after breakfast she would paint
and I would write
and as the spring rain fell on the skylight
and the tea steamed from its mugs
my heart hummed
to the music
of the dream
we'd found.

IT'S ALWAYS SAFE
TO DO NOTHING
WHEN IT RAINS.

There is no safer place I know
than tucked
in a corner
of a café in Paris
with a bottle of rosé
and an afternoon to spare.

To the poet every curve of her was a well-placed word.

A muse
is a love affair
between
art
and souls.

The sunset seeped off the Seine

dripping down our shoulders and fingers

in the oranges of the Musée d'Orsay

cigarette smoke danced in the scattering light

as if in symphony

with the orchestra of some far-off conductor

to fall and rise and fall at once—

the light lilting to our laughs

splitting into a thousand pieces

and we were caught in the center of it

hung among the stars

suspended in the disco ball of space.

Some moments
like some people
are not meant
to be fully understood
so for now
it's best
we just call them miracles.

STARS

Ma luciole
my firefly
the very spark of my life
in the darkest night
burning bright
you are my hope
the only light I need
to see.

ATTICUS

20

Red wine is good for
your complexion
it breaks you out
in smiles.

There is no excuse

I've heard

worthy

to decline

a request

by a lady of

reasonable

morals

and pleasant

company

for a skinny dip

under a warm

summer moon.

Let's
burn
bridges
and dance
naked
on
our
island.

TEACH ME THAT MUSIC

THAT FLOWS

BENEATH

YOUR SKIN.

Even eyes can sing
when properly listened to.

Mon cœur

my heart

you are missing from me

as noticeably

as if I woke

without a leg

so far away

you beat

that I must hobble

through my day

missing you with

missing pieces.

Wine tastes sweeter when drunk on love in Paris.

We loved each other in French
passing notes
we could barely read
but it didn't matter
our love was alive
breathing there
between the lines.

A good
poet paints
the pictures
we have in our minds
with colors
we didn't know
were there.

I've always loved lavender,
it's purple in all the right places.

You weren't given wings
to see the world from a tree.

Give like the sun
and the
whole world
grows tall.

It's hard to be mad at the world
nearby the miracle
of a hummingbird's wings.

YOU

ARE

ALL

THE

BEST

PARTS

ABOUT

THE

RAIN.

ATTICUS

We lost ourselves

eyes shut in a kiss

our lips the thread

that held us to the earth like a balloon

while we floated in the cosmic cotton of space

toes dipping in the pools of black

cooling our bodies—

until we awoke

in wet wool

in the rain of real

the mists of morning

soaking in a park

so cold but warm with you

and

only the rain

to remind us we

were there at all.

We collided by mistake
fate dancing
in the rafters
as I wandered
the room
until I saw you
laughing to a friend
and I
closed my eyes
so I could see
the white swing
the children laughing
a thousand moments
of happy
and sad
and old hands
in old hands
a life in a flash
and there,
in my open eyes—
was you.

The world slowed its spin
in awe of love
like cars slowing for an accident
but instead of a fire
there was just you and I
kissing on a bridge in June.

An open window in Paris
is all the world I need.

We disappeared into old bookshops
down hidden cobbled streets
the kind you had to get lost to find
each puddle jump
taking us further from
the world we'd left behind.

Write about me
she said—
for what's the use
in loving a poet
if they don't
make you
live forever.

47

Girls are like jazz to me
a kind of mixed-up magic music
unpredictable but right
as if the notes
however random
were chosen perfectly
for that moment
so that when you close your eyes
you can't help but smile
and tap your foot
to the way they make you feel.

I owe her a lot of my inspiration
but I also owe coffee
and I had to quit both
for reasons of the heart.

Distance is a
dangerous tool of desire
that must be carefully dosed
should it become
permanent.

Today
I found an old book
on my shelves
I opened the pages
and smelled the smells
and for a moment
my mind forgot its place and time
as I walked into a cabin
so many miles and years away—
there was a fire on
and the kettle played its tune.
The sun was shining
and my family was there
waving me down to the beach—
I can't tell you
how incredible it is
to be there now
writing to you
from the cabin of my youth.

A troubled youth
burnt me alive
the poet came from the ashes
the words came from the fire.

Alone in the coldest dark
a fire is a smiling friend
walking out of the shadows.

Too many die
with a brush in their hands
a heart full of colors
and a lifetime of empty canvases.

STARS

Everything
we love
is just
well-
arranged
dust.

ATTICUS

57

It rained in Rome
but when the sun came out
it seemed fresh
like a city made new
and the ruins glimmered
reminding me
that nothing lasts forever
not cities
not kingdoms
not rainstorms.

Art has the answers
to many
of the questions
we weren't brave
enough to ask.

Europe clogged my heart
with all the joys of life
the only cure
the doctor said
was to cleanse myself
completely
of any culture,
inspiration,
or authenticity,
so he prescribed
a healthy
but not deadly dose
of Hollywood.

Poets are souls at war with words
from battles waged within.

Sometimes,

to be alone is the best company.

ATTICUS

The right muse
will inspire
truth
over
imagination.

The doubters
are just dreamers
with broken hearts.

And the little girl smiled,

'Sunset,'

she said,

'that is my favorite color.'

ALL POETS
HAVE THE MODEST
ASPIRATION
THAT THEIR WORDS
WILL LIVE FOREVER.

ATTICUS

I have seen comets fall in the black skies of a desert night

I have made wishes on the wind with princes and kings

I have made love to you in the scarlet blanket of a sunset in
Spain

I am tired from a life so lived

give me now the long sleep

and I will say to you—

'Good night, my love, good night.'

ATTICUS

71

Come on darling
she said
let's drink wine
and paint
our universe.

BETWEEN

Let there be spaces in your togetherness and let the
winds of the heavens dance between you. Love one
another but make not a bond of love: let it rather be
a moving sea between the shores of your souls.

—KHALIL GIBRAN

The day I met you I began
to forget a life without you.

I'm tired
of
their stories
let's write
our own

'What if she says no?'
asked the boy,
and the old man smiled,
'best not live scared of thorns
or you'll never find a rose.'

BETWEEN|

SHE WAS NO ONE

TO ME

ON A TRAIN IN MAY

AND EVERYONE

TO ME

UNDER THE STARS IN JUNE.

ATTICUS

80

*I fell in love
with
that strange
world
she was.*

I race to fall asleep with you
to meet you
in the morning
a little more in love each day.

You set aflame
in my heart and mind
the most beautiful chaos.

Don't stir us from this champagne slumber—
let us dream a little longer in this infancy of love.

I want to know every part of you,
every scar,
every bruise,
I want to trace the map of you,
my fingers a compass,
your freckles the constellations
which in my heart I will chart
so when I close my eyes
I'll have you in my stars forever.

The problem with falling in love
is that everything else in life
becomes boring by comparison.

She wore the moonlight,

as if

the universe,

which so rarely worked in *perfects*,

had let this one

slip through.

SHE

WAS JUST

ANOTHER

GIRL

PLAYING

HOPSCOTCH

WITH

THE STARS.

Your sweet laugh
wanders through
my mind
tiptoeing whispers
for my heart to find.

I'm glad I found you

because

before you

I never knew what to wish for.

Every night

I'd come to bed

and she'd be

turned around in some magnificent position

that only the most purely asleep could find

and every time

I'd take a picture

filled with the overwhelming desire

to never forget how much I loved the way she dreamed.

Our minds follow

well behind

the old magic of our souls

that knows it's

in love

from the first moment

we see them.

She was like
that smell of a campfire
burning
in the distance
warming you
from far away.

You feel right
to me,
she said,
like naked
on cashmere.

If we were caught

in a snowstorm

in a tent

on the side of a mountain

and things were looking grim

she was the kind of girl

who would smile

bundle close to me

and say something like

Let's sing a Christmas song.

EVERY MOMENT SPENT WITH HER
I BECOME A LITTLE MORE SURE
ANYTHING IS POSSIBLE.

ATTICUS

101

She
was
just
my
kind
of
crazy.

She was one of the rare ones
so effortlessly herself
and the world loved her for it.

Loving him
was like sinking into a warm bath
lying there in the soft safety of his silence.

Her love
happened to me a hundred times at once,
in a thousand different ways,
as a million different colors.

She sipped the air
after the rain
and it tickled
her nose
like sweet
champagne.

She stole my heart
with a lip graze on an earlobe
lingered on a whisper
'don't leave.'

Her love came from deep within

a calm acceptance

of who she was in the world

a quiet respect

for the face

she saw

in the mirror.

'Girls,'
the old man said,
'are an ever-flowing music—
no use complaining about the song,
just find one
that makes you want to dance.'

ATTICUS

Our lovers fascinate us—
we live in perpetual awe
of the particular way they are.

Don't wake her
let her sleep a little longer
tucked beneath
the crimson wool of morning
with only the slight
flicker of her eyelids
left to linger
in her last dreams.

I LOVE YOU MOST IN THAT PLACE
BETWEEN COFFEE AND SLEEP.

She was the dream
I had been searching for,
the one to
wake me up.

Take away
my days
and nights
but leave me forever
mornings
with those
hazel eyes.

BETWEEN|

My love for her
became the constant
against which I
measured truth.

120

There are
magnets in my
bones for
the iron
in her blood.

'Well,'
her mother said,
'now you've done it
you've kissed off
more than you can marry.'

Twice
I would die
for a little more
once
with you.

*The problem with loving crazy
is that crazy starts to rub off.*

Sometimes
it's the ones
we only meet
in moments
that stay
with us the longest
never diluted
by the imperfections of reality
but forever perfect
in the quiet fade of memory.

Our love

was not

meant to be

it would stay forever

as unsent letters

dusting

in the quiet basements

of our hearts.

You wore a smile and a scar
in the front seat
of an old Cadillac
we were two kids chasing sunsets
holding on to memories in moments—
all the ways you were
I wish I could've bottled it up
that feeling
drinking it now that
you are gone.

She remained in me
as memories
released at random
as warm nostalgia
or terrible anxiety.

If love could have saved us
we would have lived forever

It sometimes takes a long time

and a hard time

to realize

he just doesn't deserve your *you*.

BETWEEN|

She lost
herself
in him
and after
he was gone
there was a great
re-finding.

ATTICUS
134

So many love letters
left on the wind,
that when the trees stir
she sees only him.

Love
the one they are
not the one
they should be.

She burrowed her face
into me,
'I missed you,'
she said,
'*long* before I ever knew you.'

Love
by its very nature
is fragile
and that's what makes
true love
so powerful—
you make a fragile thing
strong.

HE SHIELDED

HER HEART

LIKE A FLAME

IN A STORM—

HIS BACK

AGAINST

THE WIND.

I love her because she steals my socks
I love her because when I find her in them
they never match
I love her because they are always too big
and the gray part for the heel sits far too high
I love her because she wears them to sleep
and one always falls off
and then she wakes in the night and can't find it
and her foot is cold—
that is why I love her.

I won't ever find the words for you—
you are my everything always
and even that is not enough.

You are
my fairy tale
my book
to never finish
let me linger
in your story
a little ever
longer.

'Do you hear that?'
he said,
'Listen close
the universe is singing to us
in shooting stars
daring us to fall in love.'

THE DARK

Though my soul may set in darkness,
it will rise in perfect light;
I have loved the stars too fondly
to be fearful of the night.

—SARAH WILLIAMS

There is all sorts of magic
beaming in your bones.

LIFE

IS THE ART

OF FAILING

MAGNIFICENTLY.

The trick is always
to *try*
collect the *tries*
like trophies
and you will
never lose.

'You are a bird,
my girl,'
her father said,
'shake the water from your feathers
spread those mighty wings
and fly.'

We will never get back the life we waste
trying to be normal.

ATTICUS

154

Put your hand on your heart
in you
there is power
there are ideas
no one has ever thought of
there is the strength to love
purely and intensely
and to be loved back
there is the power to make people happy
and to make people laugh
the power to change lives
and futures
don't ever forget that power
and don't ever
give up on it.

It is so easy to forget
we are the same as all the others
in thinking that we are different.

Have you ever looked at the stars drunk
and sworn they were burning just for you?
It's hard not to believe in magic
it's hard not to believe in whiskey.

The earth was drunk
and it stumbled along
as I walked
steadily home from the bar.

It's a good night for whiskey
there's something about the rain
that makes me want to burn.

'Stay away from trouble,'
momma said
but then
some of us need
the storm to feel safe.

CHAMPAGNE IS A TRADE OF GOOD
TIMES FOR HEADACHES.

Death is the only adventure I have patience for

I love those laughs
that come from deep within
the kind that are catching to anyone close
that make your stomach hurt
and cry with tears of joy
the kind that come
when you least expect
where the more you try to stop
the harder it becomes
and even when you think of them now
you smile—
those are the laughs
of real old
human magic.

Have you ever
smelled a smell
that brings you
instantly back
to a moment
from your youth?
I always loved that feeling.
I hope that's what death is
just sitting on clouds
smelling old smells.

ATTICUS

The funny thing
about chasing the past
is that most
people
wouldn't know
what to do
if they caught it.

ATTICUS
◆

Down in the cellar were
A hundred dusty bottles
from a hundred different years
We'd open barrels to spill
just enough for a glass
The red would drip down the oak
and with our fingers we'd feel the wood
and the wetness of the wine
and for a moment the world would warm
and we'd know somewhere in that feeling
was life as it was intended.

Never believe
old men or
politicians
on issues
that will make
them wealthier
while they are alive
and the world
worse when they
are dead.

ATTICUS
◆
171

Some days life is a grand adventure,
other days it seems
an uncomfortable necessity between sleeps.

I hate to be alone
there are too many voices talking.

The problem with dating these days
is that we compare real humans
to the perfect potential
of everyone we haven't met yet.

ATTICUS
176

Don't worry
if someone
doesn't love you
sometimes
they are
struggling first
to love themselves.

A soul mate would be great,

but at some point

I'd settle for someone who gets back to text messages.

THE DARK|

She loved him with everything she had
but somewhere along the way
she forgot that she too was someone,
she too was worth loving.

THE DARK

I let her go
she was a bird I had caged
that had forgotten how to fly
but dreamed of clouds
when she closed her eyes.

Don't waste any more tomorrows
on someone who wastes your todays.

NEVER

BE AFRAID

TO CHANGE

THE PRINCE'S NAME

IN YOUR

STORY.

You must
let the love
for yourself
set you
free of them.

She had survived
his love
and with the embers
he left behind
she lit the
mighty
flames of
her future.

'Keep your head up,'
the old man said,
'for you are a lion
don't forget that
and neither
will the sheep.'

The plane shook
and it scared her
not because she
was scared to fall
but because she cared
so little
if she did.

In all probability
there is a person out there
that is almost exactly the same
as the one you just lost,
except that they are a little bit taller,
a little bit kinder,
and a whole lot better in bed.

She didn't know why she did it,

she felt trapped inside her skin,

and maybe,

she thought,

just maybe,

the cuts would let the light in.

The truth is
sometimes
you can
both
do better.

Sometimes we
feed the hurt
inside us
like a wild bear on a chain
just to see
how angry we can make it
before letting it go.

As he chased demons
born in youth
all I could do was watch
with a jealous curiosity
for the fire he fed with drink
what a marvelous,
inspiring, terrible thing
to live so close
to madness.

We sip the poison
our minds pour
      for us
and wonder
why we feel so sick.

She wore a thousand faces
all to hide her own.

She walked
through life
with the eyes
of a wolf
who belonged to no one
but the night.

She was powerful
not because she wasn't scared
but because
she went on so strongly
despite the fear.

Her courage was her crown
and she wore it like a queen.

The bravest thing
she ever did
was to stay alive
each day.

YOU ARE

ENOUGH,

A THOUSAND

TIMES

ENOUGH.

Courage is getting on a bull
knowing no matter how well you ride
you're getting thrown at the end.

We all wear scars—
find someone
who makes yours
feel beautiful.

Alone we live short rebellions of death,
together we defy it.

Stay alive,
tomorrow
is there
for those
that wait.

There is not enough time in life
to worry about there not being enough time in life.

There was always
something magic
in the way
she was
in the rain.

'Silly girl,'
the old lady laughed,
'your
different
is
your
beautiful.'

To be alive
is the strange
and wondrous miracle
we forget.

We are human
bold & brilliant
and we will rise *always*
from the ashes of our doubt
to wield our differences
not as a weakness
but as swords
to take our beauty back.

You are worth your imperfections
you are worth your bad days
you are worth your good
you are worth your confusion
you are worth your insecurities
you are worth fighting for
and you are worth loving.
And that's a fck'ing fact.

The sunset raged
in its gentle fury
a four-horsed apocalypse
charging toward us
huddled on a beach
in woolen blankets
singing songs
on a ukulele
to the ever-riding doom of dark.